Exploring Materials

Rubber

Abby Colich

Heinemann
LIBRARY
Chicago, Illinois

To contact Capstone Global Library please phone 800-747-4992, or
visit our website www.capstonepub.com

Edited by Abby Colich, Daniel Nunn, and Catherine Veitch
Designed by Marcus Bell
Picture research by Tracy Cummins
Production by Victoria Fitzgerald
Originated by Capstone Global Library Ltd

Library of Congress Cataloging-in-Publication Data
Colich, Abby.
  Rubber / Abby Colich.
    pages cm.—(Exploring materials)
  Includes bibliographical references and index.
  ISBN 978-1-4329-8019-1 (hb)—ISBN 978-1-4329-8027-6 (pb) 1.
Rubber—Juvenile literature. I. Title.

  TS1890.C67 2014
  678'.2—dc23   2012047535

Acknowledgments
The author and publisher are grateful to the following for permission
to reproduce copyright material: Getty Images: Goh Seng Chong/
Bloomberg, 9, Jay P. Morgan, 7, LWA/Dann Tardif, Cover, Tuan Tran, 4;
Shutterstock: AISPIX by Image Source, 17, Anatoli Styf, 8, ArtmannWitte,
13, Blazej Lyjak, 10, 23, Blend Images, 21, Cheryl Casey, 6 top left,
daniaphoto, 6 bottom right, Diego Cervo, 18, fred goldstein, 6 bottom
left, Jeannette Meier Kamer, 16, Maridav, 19, 23, Marie C Fields, 6 top
right, Neale Cousland, 22 top right, Olegusk, 15, Scott Alan Photo, 22
top left, stoykovic, 12, Vitaly Korovin, 22 bottom, Vitaly Titov, 5, Vladimir
Melnik, Back Cover, 11; SuperStock: ImageSource, 20, Juice Images,
14

We would like to thank Valarie Akerson, Nancy Harris, Dee Reid,
and Diana Bentley for their invaluable help in the preparation of
this book.

Every effort has been made to contact copyright holders of any
material reproduced in this book. Any omissions will be rectified in
subsequent printings if notice is given to the publisher.

Contents

What Is Rubber?

Rubber is a material.

Materials are what things are made from.

Many things are made from rubber.

Rubber has many different uses.

Where Does Rubber Come From?

rubber

Some rubber comes from trees.

Some rubber is made by people.

Rubber can be recycled or reused.

Recycled rubber can be used to make new things.

What Is Rubber Like?

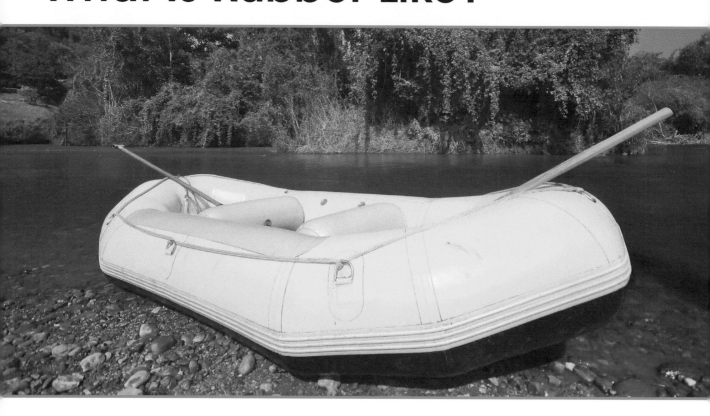

Rubber can be soft.

Rubber can be hard.

Rubber can bounce.

Rubber can stretch.

How Do We Use Rubber?

Tires are made of rubber.

Some toys are made of rubber.

Rubber gloves protect our hands.

Rubber boots protect our feet.

rubber

We use rubber at school.

swimming cap

We use rubber when we exercise.

Quiz

a

b

c

Which of these things are made from rubber?

Answer on page 24.

Picture Glossary

protect keep safe. Rubber boots keep feet safe from getting wet.

recycle make used items into new things

Index

The **flip-flops (a)** and **glove (c)** are made from rubber.

Notes for Parents and Teachers
Before reading
Ask children if they have heard the term "material" and what they think it means. Reinforce the concept of materials. Explain that all objects are made from different materials. A material is something that takes up space and can be used to make other things. Ask children to give examples of different materials. These may include glass, plastic, and rubber.

To get children interested in the topic, ask if they know what rubber is. Identify any misconceptions they may have. Ask them to think about whether their ideas might change as the book is read.

After reading
• Check to see if any of the identified misconceptions have changed.
• Show the children examples of rubber, including rubber bands, erasers, and a rubber toy.
• Pass the rubber objects around. Ask the children to describe the properties of each object. Is the object heavy or light? Does it bounce or stretch? What are the colors? Ask them to name other items made from rubber.